MW01519408

ALEX & THE DATA BUGS

Written and Illustrated By
Robin Herst Rose

Dedicated to Hadley Rose, Ron Herst
and to my sons Lucas M.W. Rose and
Zachary Alexander Rose.

Publisher's Cataloging-in-Publication Data
Rose, Robin Herst, author, illustrator. Title: ALEX & THE DATA BUGS.
Summary: While waiting for his mom to take him to the park, Alex discovers a new creative outlet for his active imagination.
Identifiers: LCCN 2019910391   ISBN 978-0-9857934-4-9 (hardcover) I ISBN 978-0-9857934-5-6 (paperback) I ISBN 978-0-9857934-6-3 (epub) I ISBN 978-0-9857934-7-0 (mobi)
Subjects: Computers and children—Juvenile fiction. I Action—Adventure Fiction.

York Street Market

Mission Entry #1
It all began on what seemed to be a typical day at our family market.

I was busy snacking, testing my acrobatic skills and listening to music when I suddenly noticed a flyer on my brother's desk: "Come and experience the thrill of flight in our new ACE PILOT ADVENTURE RIDE—Visit Larksberry Park TODAY!"

Wow! That sounded really amazing! I'd always dreamed about flying around in my own jet plane, so I couldn't wait to go there and try it out.

I ran into the kitchen where Chef Marchello was assembling his yummy looking culinary creations and asked, "Have you seen Mom? I really need her to take me to Larksberry Park—right now!"

"Oh, no, no, no," he said. "Your mother is working on the computer, adding my latest appetizer inventions to our Party-To-Go menu. I have created the tastiest, most delicious little morsels for our customers. No, Alex, you mustn't disturb your mother now. That menu must be updated and printed today! No, immediately!"

"Okay, thanks Chef Marchello," I said as I ran upstairs to the office.

"Mom, Mom, can you take me to Larksberry Park?"

"We can go as soon as I figure out what's going wrong with our new business program. Letters and even whole words are disappearing from our Party-To-Go menu. It must be some kind of data bug!"

What? A real bug... alive inside our computer? Awesome! But I wanted to help, so I wondered if I could somehow trap it and put it outside—where bugs belong.

I ran into the kitchen to find some kind of data bug food. Then I saw it— chips! Everyone loves chips! I grabbed a handful and ran back to the office.

"Alex! What in the world are you doing?"

"Mom, the data bug is going to come out to eat these chips, and then I'll get him, and then we can go to the park!" I replied confidently.

We ate the chips as Mom explained to me that the data bug doesn't come out. It causes problems inside the computer. She then said, "Don't worry Alex, it probably won't take very long to fix this. I'll call for you when I'm ready to go."

Angry that I now had to wait to go to the park, but needing something to do to pass the time, I looked on my shelf of books and games. Bored with all my old stuff, I suddenly spotted the unopened gift Chef Marchello had given me.

THE MAGIC ELECTRO PEN and MISSION LOG NOTEBOOK
You now have THE POWER, THE DEVICE and THE MAGIC to make the impossible—possible! Just enter your wish and make it come true! Lead the way and start a fun new adventure today!

I opened the box, slowly lifted the pen and wrote: I wish I could go *inside* our computer and DESTROY that data bug! Then, I pressed the ENTER button. Instantly a swirl of clouds streamed out of the pen, and a strong wind *wooshed* me off my feet!

Surrounded by spinning clouds, I saw distant flashes of lightning and exploding sparks of brightly colored lights. The air cleared as my feet touched down, and to my amazement, there I was—inside the computer and standing right on the Party-To-Go menu! "It worked—it worked!" I shouted.

Suddenly I heard a loud C-r-rack! Then a hummm...Crunch, Crunch, Crunch. C-r-rack! hummm...Crunch, Crunch, Crunch.

I snuck in a little closer and...

NACHOS
CHEESE PUFF
GORGONZOLA
CHEDDA
STUFF
CURB

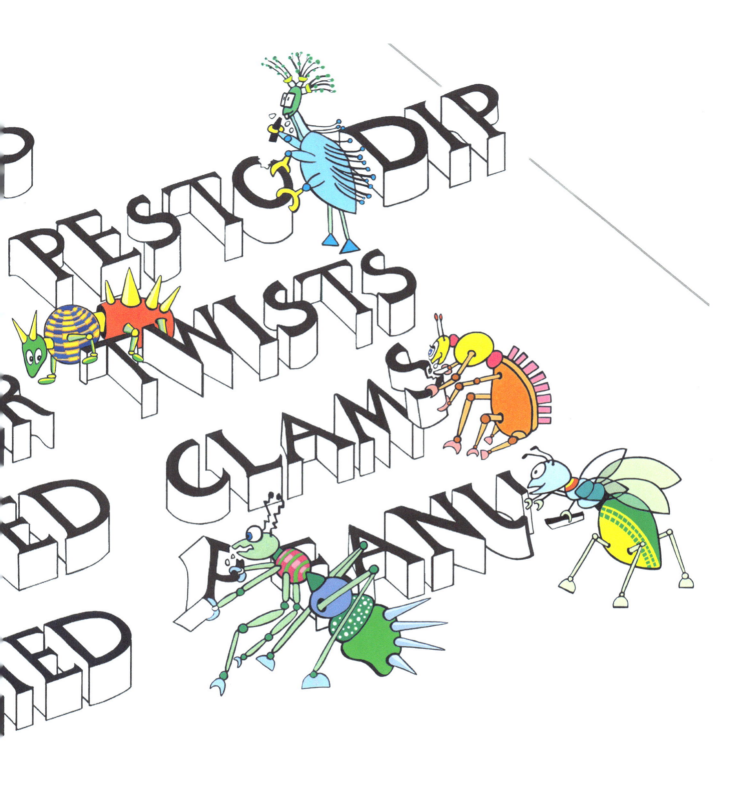

Oh my gosh! There wasn't just one data bug—there were lots!

And they were *eating* the letters and even C-r-rack - Crunch, Crunching down whole words!

I hid behind a bunch of balloons that I grabbed from the menu. Slowly sneaking away, I wondered, YIKES!—how am I ever going to destroy all of these data bugs? But lost in thought, and not looking where I was going, I suddenly fell right off the edge of the page! "Oh Noooooo!"

Luckily, the balloons floated me to a super soft landing onto the page below. Where was I now? As I looked around, all at once I realized that I was in a greeting card website! The same exact website that we used to send my grandpa an animated birthday card!

While looking at all the fun cards, I remembered that when we were choosing grandpa's card Mom had said to me, "Alex, stop clicking on all the cards. The computer will freeze if there are too many things open at the same time."

Hmmmm.....

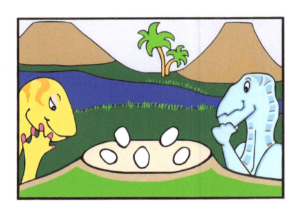

the computer will f r e e z e if there are too many things open at the same time. That's it! I've got it! Freeze the computer! I'll click open a bunch of these animating cards, the computer will overload and freeze, and the data bugs will freeze too! That's it! Thats it!

Okay! Watch out all you little buggers! Mission Computer Freeze—here I come!

I quickly put on some warm clothes that I picked up from a nearby card, because I knew that when the computer freezes, it was definitely going to get very, very, cold!

Next, I needed to move the cursor to open the cards, but just as I lifted my hand the cursor magically followed to wherever I pointed. I hopped on top, pointed and yelled,   *"GO-GO-GO!"*

I zoomed in, landed on the first card and Click—it began to animate, then off I flew to the next and...

Click—animated the second. Click—began the third. "Yippee, this is so much fun!" I shouted. But just as I was clicking open the fourth card, I lost my balance and fell off the cursor and into the animating birthday card below!!!

"Ah h h h h h h h h h h!"

HAPPY BIRTHDAY

Then—Crash! Bang! Bang!
Everything stopped moving! Then suddenly...

HAPPY BIRTHDAY

Everything froze!
The animating cards turned off and the screen turned blue!

'WOO HOO!" I shouted.
"The circuits inside the data bugs are freezing and cracking apart!
I did it! I did it! I destroyed the data bugs!"

Over the sounds of the crackling of freezing data bugs came the roar of incoming planes. It was the Computer Security Police Patrol!

The planes landed and the security police packed the data bugs in freezer bags marked:
Defrost
Repair and Reprogram.

One of the officers came up to me and shook my hand and said, "Well done young man! Thank you for finding and stopping those destructive little critters before they did any further damage." The officer then took a shiny gold medal out of his pocket, pinned it on my coat and said, "You are now a member of our Junior Computer Security Squad."

Wow! I sure felt proud.

With my mission successfully completed, it was time to go, so I took the Magic Electro Pen out of my pocket and pressed the HOME button and... *woosh*... there I was, back at my desk.

Fun gift Chef Marchello, I thought as I finished logging in my first adventure.

"A L E X," called Mom, "I've finished printing the menu, let's go to the park!"

So, I finally got to Larksberry Park and...

I happily hopped inside the new... the incredible...
ACE PILOT ADVENTURE RIDE!
And flew off on my next amazing Magic Electro Mission.

CPSIA information can be obtained
at www.ICGtesting.com
Printed in the USA
LVHW070027041120
670657LV00022B/1199